The Revelation of Jesus

Crystal

The Revelation of Jesus

Seeing Christ in Others

Tom Tiemens

Unless otherwise indicated, all scriptural quotations are from the King James Version of the Bible.

Scripture quotations marked (AMP) are taken from The Amplified Bible, Old Testament. Copyright ©1965, 1987 by The Zondervan Corporation. The Amplified New Testament, copyright ©1954, 1958, 1987 by The Lockman Foundation. Used by permission.

Scripture quotations marked NKJV are from The New King James Version. Copyright ©1979, 1980, 1982, Thomas Nelson Inc., Publishers. Used by permission.

The Revelation of Jesus: Seeing Christ in Others
by Tom Tiemens
ISBN 0-88270-723-X
Library of Congress Catalog Card Number:96-84799
Copyright © 1996 by **BRIDGE-LOGOS** *Publishers*

Published by:
BRIDGE-LOGOS *Publishers*
North Brunswick Corporate Center
1300 Airport Road, Suite E
North Brunswick, NJ 08902

Printed in the United States of America.
All rights reserved.
Under International Copyright Law, no part of this publication may be reproduced, stored, or transmitted by any means—electronic, mechanical, photographic (photocopy), recording, or otherwise—without written permission from the Publisher.

Table of Contents

Introduction vii

1. The Revelation of Jesus Christ 1

2. Looking Through a Glass Darkly 11

3. The Unveiling of Jesus Christ 21

4. Healing Broken Relationships 29

5. The New Commandment 37

6. The Benefits of Fellowship 49

7. Visions of Jesus 55

8. Love Never Fails 73

Introduction

> That I may know him, and the power of his resurrection, and the fellowship of his sufferings, being made conformable unto his death.
> Philippians 3:10

    I appreciate what Paul says here. I appreciate the kind of heart I see reflected in this verse. Paul's greatest desire was for Jesus Christ to be revealed. The cry of his heart was for intimate knowledge of the Son of God.

    Several months ago the Lord spoke to me and said that in these last days He is going to raise up a people who love Jesus Christ supremely; a people who have an uncommon love for the Son of God. I want to be that kind of man—a Jesus person, a man having an unfailing love for and faith in the Lord Jesus Christ.

    God is raising up a people in these last days who have no fascination for the world. They have tried the cisterns of this life and found them empty. The world with all its glitter and its glamour was never able to satisfy the craving and emptiness of their soul.

So they have turned their back on the world. They have said, "The world has no claim on me." Their allegiance is to Jesus Christ alone. Now they are saying, "Lord, no price is too great. If serving You will cost me my life, then I bring my life to You at this moment. My soul lays claim to the Lordship of Jesus Christ."

That's the kind of man and woman Jesus Christ is raising up in these last days—not just disciples in word, but disciples in deed.

Through the years, I have been fortunate to become acquainted with wonderful men and women of God; people who have touched me and blessed my life. One such man is a great missionary-evangelist whom my wife, Shelvia, and I are privileged to know. We consider him to be our spiritual mentor, and we have him preach at our church in Fresno, California, as often as he can come.

The Chinese Underground Church

My friend told about an experience he'd had in Red China, where he met members of the Chinese underground church. He said, "I've never before met men and women like this. The dedication I found in those people brought conviction to my life. Many from the ranks have been put to death because they would not deny the name of Jesus Christ."

He told me that these men and women had fasted— not for days, but for weeks—anticipating his visit. Recognizing the life this great missionary has lived and what he has meant to the nations of the Earth over the last 60 years, these Chinese believers fasted and prayed so they might fully receive the Word of God that fell from his lips.

Purity and Dedication

My friend said, "When I looked into the faces of those Chinese believers, I was humbled. I was convicted. I turned my face from them. I could not look at the purity and the dedication of their lives. I have found no believers, no group of Christians, like them anywhere else on the face of the Earth."

Then he told about the miracles that are taking place in Red China. He said, "The dead are being raised. The works of Jesus are taking place in that nation."

When I heard about these Chinese Christians, I became convicted in my heart, and I found myself saying, "O God, what about North America? What about the Western world?"

We need Christians in the United States, Canada, Europe, Africa, Central and South America, Australia, and New Zealand like the Christians who are living behind the Bamboo Curtain in Red China.

The Blood-Bought Church

I believe with all my heart that God is in the process of raising up a Church like that in the Western world. I've prayed and asked the Lord to help me be the man He wants me to be and the kind of Christian He has called me to be. I want to be a part of that blood-bought Church that will not deny the Lord Jesus Christ.

I want Jesus filling every nook and cranny, every room in my spiritual house. I refuse to close a door to Him. And everything in me that is not like Jesus I want burned up in the fire of the love of God. Our God is a consuming fire!

The cry of my heart is, "Lord, consume everything in me—every thought, attitude, and desire—that is not consistent with Jesus Christ. May I stand before Him without reproof and without rebuke in His love."

Empty Cisterns

I, too, have tried to drink from the world's cisterns. There is no refreshing water in them. I have tried the things of the natural life. They only create a spiritual life that is bankrupt and empty. My cry is for the revelation and the intimate knowledge of the Son of God to me and through me. And I declare this before Jesus Christ and His holy Father: "Lord Jesus, I will know You, and I will walk in the knowledge of You, the Son of God!"

By God's grace and with His help, I will be the person He has called me to be, and I pray this same prayer for you as well. May your heart be so gripped by the love of God and the revelation of Jesus Christ that you are changed into the likeness of Christ.

Jesus is coming! The Father is sending Jesus for a Church that looks like Himself—a Church that is a perfect mirror, a perfect reflection, of the Son of God.

We are being changed into His likeness and glory. We are moving from glory to glory, from strength to strength, and from faith to faith. My earnest prayer is that you and I be found worthy to be a part of that glorious Church!

Tom Tiemens
Fresno, California - 1995

1

The Revelation of Jesus Christ

I'm convinced that all Christians can love Jesus a little more than they do right now. That's where the message of this book is going to take us—into a greater realm of the love of God.

As 1 Corinthians 2:9-11 says, our eyes have not seen, our ears have not heard, and our hearts have not known the surpassing majesty and loveliness of Jesus Christ. After reading this book, may our hearts comprehend, to a much greater degree than they do now, how very wonderful He is.

I am convinced that if people can see Jesus, they will desire Him; and in desiring Him, they will become like Him.

To get the maximum benefit from studying this book and to grow in the intimate knowledge of Jesus Christ, you must embrace what the Lord says in His Word.

Each time you embrace a line of truth that God is attempting to add to your life, it allows you to embrace subsequent lines of truth.

People have come to me through the years saying things like, "Pastor, I haven't heard the Lord speak for a long time." They don't realize when they make that statement that they're telling me a great deal about their spiritual life.

They're saying, "At some point in time, I heard the Lord speak to me, and I answered this way: 'Lord, tomorrow I'll do that,' or, 'One day I'll do that,' or, 'Lord, this is a hard thing You're asking of me.'" They said "no" to the voice of God, and they stopped growing because of it.

Joy in Serving Jesus

Jesus said, "My yoke is easy, and my burden is light." Serving Jesus is not a grievous thing; it's a wonderful, joyful thing!

There is a 'spout' where the glory of the Lord is indeed poured out, and you will find that the 'spout' for your life is in doing the will of God. The will of God is the predetermined purpose of God for your life. He has called *you* to do something unique. He has not called you to do what He has called me to do. If we refuse to walk in the will of God for our lives, that part of the will of God goes undone.

God is not going to raise up another man or woman to do what He has called you to do. When we stand before the Judgment Seat of Christ one day, we will each answer to the Lord according to His plan and purpose for *our* life. (I know those are sobering words, but they need to be stated.)

There is great joy in serving Jesus Christ. There is great peace in the heart of the person who knows he is absolutely one with the plan and purpose of God for his life.

John's Vision of Jesus

The Lord Jesus—the resurrected and glorified Christ—appeared to the apostle John on the island of Patmos. John did not see, however, the Jesus whom he had seen on the streets of Jerusalem nor the Jesus whom he had seen on the shores of the Sea of Galilee.

Instead, he saw the Jesus who sits at the right hand of God and ever lives to make intercession for you and me—the glorified Christ!

This is how John described our glorified Lord:

> His head and his hairs were white like wool, as white as snow; and his eyes were as a flame of fire;
>
> and his feet like unto fine brass, as if they burned in a furnace; and his voice as the sound of many waters.
>
> And he had in his right hand seven stars: and out of his mouth went a sharp two-edged sword: and his countenance was as the sun shineth in his strength.
>
> And when I saw him, I fell at his feet as dead.
> Revelation 1:14-17

John was so overcome by what he saw, so paralyzed by fright, he fell at the Lord's feet as if dead. Jesus told him not to be afraid, and He gave him seven letters to write to the seven churches in Asia Minor.

Those seven churches actually existed at that time in history. As I have carefully studied Jesus' letters to them, I have found prophetic parallels to the modern Church.

For example, the seventh church—the last one—was the church at Laodicea, a church that looks a lot like the Church in the Western world.

Many Christians in our country have no more than "Sunday-morning Christianity," but Jesus wants to change that. I believe with all my heart that God is committed to changing the face of Christianity in our nation over the next few years.

Fighting Spiritual Doldrums

When I took a group of men from our church on a missions trip to India, I warned them they might feel spiritual doldrums upon returning to the United States, because the overwhelming spiritual hunger found on the foreign field is not always found in U.S. churches.

I remember the first time I went to India. I preached in a crusade outside the city of Shillong. I was told that some people had started walking at 4 a.m. to be in our 10 o'clock service that morning. It was little wonder we saw miracles that paralleled those in the Book of Acts. The people paid a price to be there.

We saw people run, not walk, to the altars to receive Jesus. We didn't have to coax or beg them, or ask them to raise their hands first and then stand up. We didn't have to ask someone to grab them by the hand and bring them. *They ran to make Jesus Christ their Lord and Savior!* There was a desperation in their hearts—a desperation you could see in their eyes.

As I stood by the pulpit, people desperate for Jesus Christ grabbed my clothing and fell at my feet, praying for the miracle of salvation.

We in the West live in such affluence compared to the rest of the world. We have so many diversions within our reach that it's easy to allow things to anesthetize our spirit to the degree that our hunger for spiritual things is lost.

This condition is not limited to the United States alone. I've traveled the Western world and found it needs a powerful visitation of God to bring forth the spiritual hunger that is so typical in a large part of the world. The things of God were never meant to take the place of God. He alone is to occupy the shrine of our heart.

Although my heart is grieved at our spiritual condition, at the same time there is a divine excitement at work in my spirit, because I know Jesus is going to answer our prayers for a mighty revival.

Wood, Hay, and Stubble

> And unto the angel of the church of the Laodiceans write; These things saith the Amen, the faithful and true witness, the beginning of the creation of God.
> Revelation 3:14

That word "beginning" means authority and ruler. Jesus is the rightful ruler of the creation of God. He owns it all—the heavens and the Earth. Every knee shall bow and every tongue shall confess that Jesus Christ is Lord of all and over all.

Jesus says in Revelation 3:15, "I know thy works." Jesus knows our works! We tend to judge outwardly, but God sees the motive in every heart. God knows why we do the things we do and say the things we say.

One day each of us will stand before Him, and the Lord Himself will put fire to our works. All the wood, all the hay, and all the stubble will be burned. And some believers will be scarcely saved—"as one escaping through the flames" (1 Corinthians 3:15, NIV).

However, if Jesus puts fire to your works and they come forth as pure gold, He will then take that gold and fashion it into a crown that He will set upon your head.

When I stand before the Lord, I want to hear Him say, "Well done, Tom Tiemens, thou good and faithful servant."

Is that *your* reason for living, loving, and ministering as you do? If so, your reward will be great in that day.

The Lord knows our works. He sees the sacrifices we make. He sees our hearts as we put our lives into service for Him and for others.

Lukewarm Christians Nauseate the Lord

Notice what He said to the Laodicean church:

> I know thy works, that thou art neither cold nor hot: I would thou wert cold or hot.
> So then because thou art lukewarm, and neither cold nor hot, I will spue thee out of my mouth.
> Revelation 3:15-16

The King James Version is tame here. If you read the original language of the Bible, you'll find the Lord saying, "I will vomit you out of my mouth (so reads also the NKJV) if you're lukewarm. I would rather have you cold, indifferent, and backslidden than lukewarm."

There's something nauseating to the Lord about lukewarm Christians. They live in the gray twilight of deception, thinking all is well when things are not well, and the Lord can't deal with them because they think they're all right.

The Lord literally says to the lukewarm Christian, "Why don't you take two steps backwards, become an icicle, and grow cold so I can deal with you again?"

When you're wrong, you know you're wrong, and you're susceptible to conviction. God can deal with a person who has allowed the coal and the ember to go out of his life. He can right the wrong in that person's life. But lukewarm Christians, because they are deceived, are unteachable.

God wants each of us to live as firebrands before Him. He wants us to be red hot in everything we say and do. He doesn't want lukewarm Christians. I've often thought about that term "lukewarm." Have you ever tasted a cup of lukewarm coffee? I would rather not drink it! I spit lukewarm coffee out of my mouth.

Maybe you've become like a cup of cold or lukewarm coffee, and it's time you put the cup of your life into the microwave or on the burner and let God add some heat, fire, and thunder to it.

The Laodiceans' Testimony

Notice what the lukewarm, deceived Laodiceans' testimony was, and notice what Jesus thought about it:

> Because thou sayest, I am rich, and increased with goods, and have need of nothing; and knowest not that thou art wretched, and miserable, and poor, and blind, and naked:
>
> I counsel thee to buy of me gold tried in the fire, that thou mayest be rich; and white raiment, that thou mayest be clothed, and that the shame of thy

nakedness do not appear, and anoint thine eyes with eyesalve, that thou mayest see.

As many as I love, I rebuke and chasten: be zealous therefore, and repent.

Revelation 3:17-19

Their testimony was, in modern terms: "We've increased on every level. We have lots of things. We've got three cars and a two-car garage. We've got this and we've got that. We're getting all we can and keeping all we get." The Laodiceans equated their prosperity to being all right spiritually.

But the Lord answered them in the above passage by saying, in effect, "You say you have need of nothing, but this is your real spiritual condition. This is what I'm looking at."

Isaiah said of the Lord, "He is the wonderful Counselor." Any counsel God gives people is wonderful. He loves us. He comes to bless, heal, and help us.

Although Jesus rebuked the Laodician church, He also promised them a tremendous blessing if they would respond to Him. That's the nature of God. If we will right the wrongs in our lives, He will bestow His blessings on us.

The Laodiceans' Pride

Let's look at affluent Laodicea. As a center of banking and commerce in the ancient world, the finances of the known world flowed into that city and region. It was also known for the garments manufactured there. It supplied clothing to the whole world.

Laodicea was also widely known for its hospitals and institutions of higher learning; in particular, for its technology in the areas of healing and treating eye diseases. The Laodiceans took pride in all their achievements, and Jesus addressed all three major achievements: their gold, their clothing, and their eyesalve.

He said, "I want you Laodiceans to obtain from Me true gold, which is faith that has been tried and proven in the fiery crucible of conflict. I want you to wear the white robes of righteousness. And I want you to apply the eyesalve of repentance, so you may see clearly and not be deceived."

According to Revelation 19:8, "the fine linen is the righteousness of saints." It's the works of Jesus Christ. And we all know the correlation of the eyesalve. Jesus was saying, "Let the Holy Spirit remove the crust away from your eyes so you can clearly see; so you can have a heart that discerns and knows the ways and the mind of God."

Then He says something in Revelation 3:19 that I appreciate so much, and I state this as a man who has felt the chastening rod of the Lord all his Christian life—I feel it today, and I want to feel it tomorrow. I pray that God will never let me come to a place in life where I don't sense the Lord chastening me. He says, "As many as I love, I rebuke and chasten." Hallelujah! God loves us, and because of that love He rebukes and chastens us.

People used to wear funny buttons with a lot of initials on them. Those letters stood for, "Please be patient because God is not finished with me yet." I am a man under construction. I have determined in my heart that I am going to depend fully on Jesus on a daily basis.

2

Looking Through a Glass Darkly

> Jesus saith unto them, Did ye never read in the scriptures, The stone which the builders rejected, the same is become the head of the corner: this is the Lord's doing, and it is marvellous in our eyes?
>
> Therefore say I unto you, The kingdom of God shall be taken from you, and given to a nation bringing forth the fruits thereof.
>
> And whosoever shall fall on this stone shall be broken: but on whomsoever it shall fall, it will grind him to powder.
>
> Matthew 21:42-44

Jesus said of the Chief Cornerstone, "The builders and the architects of Jewish society are going to reject the Chief Cornerstone, that stone that comes down from God; and because of it, that stone is going to grind them. They will come under divine judgment."

In 70 A.D., the Roman emperor, Titus, ordered, "Destroy Jerusalem!" That period marked the beginning of the great *Diaspora* (scattering) of the Jewish people.

Jews were carried away to every nation. They left as outcasts, hidden away in the nations of the Earth. They lost their homeland because they rejected their Messiah.

When Jesus came to Earth initially, He did not come to the Gentile nations—He came as the Jewish Messiah, seeking the lost sheep of the house of Israel. But they would not have Him.

Jesus wept over them and their capital, Jerusalem. He longed to gather them "as a hen gathers her chicks," but He could not, because they refused to accept Him as their expected Messiah (Matthew 23:37). Then judgment fell on them.

God wants us to fall on Him. He doesn't want to crush us. He wants us, of our own volition, to fall on Him and be broken so the life of Christ can find expression through us. So that through us Christ can come as a revelation to lost and dying people.

The choice is ours—either we fall on Jesus, or the Rock will crush us. Thank God, He's willing to chasten us and bring us to a place of broken submission. In His great mercy He wants to spare us from judgment.

The Chastening of the Lord

The writer of Hebrews says to people who endure chastening:

> . . . ye have forgotten the exhortation which speaketh unto you as unto children, My son, despise not thou the chastening of the Lord, nor faint when thou art rebuked of him:

> For whom the Lord loveth he chasteneth, and scourgeth every son whom he receiveth.
>
> If ye endure chastening, God dealeth with you as with sons; for what son is he whom the father chasteneth not?
>
> But if ye be without chastisement, whereof all are partakers, then are ye bastards, and not sons.
>
> Hebrews 12:5-8

This kind of message doesn't cause people to shout with joy, but my job is not to make people happy; my job is to help them. And if I help them now, they will be happy later. I like what A. W. Tozer once wrote, "If on this earth I have to choose between truth and happiness, I will choose truth everytime—for I will have an eternity in which to be happy."

Spankings aren't fun, are they? Do you remember the spankings you received as a child? I certainly do! As we saw in Revelation 3:19, Jesus said, "As many as I love, I rebuke and chasten: be zealous therefore, and repent." Because God loves us, He chastens us. He chastens us so we won't be judged with the world.

Whenever you see the Lord coming to you with His chastening rod in hand, don't run from Him—run to Him! Jump up into Father's arms. That's a good place to live—in Father's arms, caressed by His love and held tightly in His arms.

Now look at the promise Jesus made the church at Laodicea. First He rebuked them, and then He said something profound and powerful to them.

The Promise to Overcomers

> Behold, I stand at the door, and knock: if any man hear my voice, and open the door, I will come in to him, and will sup with him, and he with me.
>
> To him that overcometh will I grant to sit with me in my throne, even as I also overcame and am set down with my Father in his throne.
>
> Revelation 3:20-21

Overcoming requires something of us. Paul put it this way: "I have fought a good fight, I have finished my course, I have kept the faith" (2 Timothy 4:7). We must fight this "good fight" because there is a real enemy out there—an enemy who comes only "to steal, and to kill, and to destroy" (John 10:10).

Ours is a spiritual fight. We don't wrestle against flesh and blood, we wrestle against principalities and powers. But don't be fearful of the fight because there is good news in all this—*all things are beneath our feet.* This is a fight we win, for it's a fight that has already been won for us by Jesus. As Paul wrote in Colossians:

> Blotting out the handwriting of ordinances that was against us, which was contrary to us, and took it out of the way, nailing it to his cross;
>
> And having spoiled principalities and powers, he made a shew of them openly, triumphing over them in it.
>
> Colossians 2:14-15

Having spoiled or vanquished those principalities and powers, Jesus made an open show of them, triumphing over them in His Cross. This is the fight we must fight, but it's a fight we ultimately win. I like fights in which I'm guaranteed of victory. When I enter this spiritual fight, I already know how it's going to turn out.

I don't care how big and bad the devil looks or sounds, he's no match for any child of God who walks in the center of God's will for his or her life.

"I Stand at the Door, and Knock"

In the third chapter of Revelation, Jesus told the Laodiceans, "Behold, I stand at the door, and knock . . ." (verse 20).

Members of the Laodicean church already knew Jesus redemptively. They could say, "Jesus is my Savior. My name has been written in the Lamb's Book of Life." They could say, "I have received the baptism of the Holy Spirit. I have been healed physically."

But Jesus wanted more than that. His heart was not satisfied with that. He was saying to them, "Don't be enamored with healing in and of itself. I want you to know the Healer—know Me. Know the Baptizer in the Holy Spirit. I am the One who gave you the gift of the Holy Spirit."

The Laodiceans were a part of Jesus' Church. But Jesus pictured Himself standing outside the door of their church, saying, "Please let me in! I'm knocking on your door. I want in."

They knew Him redemptively. He wanted them to know Him intimately.

Twenty centuries have come and gone—and Jesus is still standing at the door of His Church wanting in. When are we going to let Him in? When are we going to operate in the intimate knowledge of the Son of God?

I believe that is the question the Holy Spirit is asking the Church in North America and around the world: "When are you going to really *know* Me?" The object of this book is to bring that to pass in our lives.

Jesus' Passionate Longing

Jesus wanted to live inside the Laodiceans—to be central to the Laodicean church—and He wants to be the same to His believers today.

Today Jesus' heart longs for you. He wants to be together with you. Jesus is coming after His people. He has a passionate longing for His people.

I can hear Him knocking, saying to us what He said to the church at Laodicea, "I'm standing at the door of your life, and I'm knocking on it. If you hear my voice and open that door, I will come in to you. We will sit together at the intimacy of a family meal, and I'll share my heart with you as you share yours with Me."

Jesus will not stop knocking until every child of God opens that door and allows Him to assume lordship of their lives. That's the quest, the cry, of the Son of God—that the Church might know Him intimately. He wants us to fellowship with Him in the intimacy of His Word, knowledge, and splendor.

Everything orbits around Jesus Christ. He will not settle for anything less than being the center of the solar system of your life. He will keep knocking and knocking and knocking until you answer the door. And, if need be, that knock at the door of your heart will become louder in these last days until it becomes thunderous.

Stop frustrating the grace of God, and allow Him into your life. Examine your life and schedule, and change it to make time for Him, because Jesus loves you too much to let you go your own way, apart from Him.

If you refuse, you may be 'history'—out of the picture. You can lose the presence of God in your life if you turn the Lord away enough times, and we all know people who have done just that.

You're already drawing your own conclusions about this. You're thinking, "Well, I know what he's going to say. He's going to talk about prayer, Bible reading, and that kind of thing."

Although I'll mention these things, that's not the direction in which we're heading. We're going to study something else—something central to understanding who Jesus Christ really is.

An Intimate Fellowship

> Behold, I stand at the door, and knock: if any man hear my voice, and open the door, I will come in to him, and will sup with him, and he with me.
>
> Revelation 3:20

The word "sup" in this verse is a pointed word, an intimate word. It provides a clue to the intimate fellowship Jesus desires.

In our culture, we tend to eat breakfast, lunch, and dinner. The Laodiceans also ate three meals a day. Their dinner meal was called "the sup." It wasn't like the first two meals of the day.

The "sup" was a time for the family; a time for intimate family gatherings. The family would sit together for hours at a time.

Dad would sit next to his son, and they would talk about the events of the day. Dad would teach his son the commandments of the Lord. Mom would share with her daughter. The husband would look lovingly at his wife and children. They would "sup" with each other.

The Laodiceans didn't have television sets to sit in front of at family meals—outside entertainment wasn't their priority, anyway. Television is probably the greatest hindrance to our spiritual and family growth.

An Intimate Relationship

We saw earlier that in Revelation 3:20 Jesus said, in effect, "Behold, I stand at your door and knock. And if you hear My voice and open that door, I'll come in to you and sup with you. I will sit together with you in the intimacy of a family meal. I will speak to you as My son, and you will speak to Me as your Father. I will speak to you as My sister, and you will speak to Me as your older Brother."

That's what Jesus wants! And that's what He is going to have. Whatever Jesus wants, He gets. So make it easy on yourself and invite Him into your innermost being to have an intimate relationship with Him.

After inviting Jesus to abide and sup with you, you will have to make some changes in your life. You will have to get rid of the things that have been hindering you in your Christian walk. And you will have to go through an attitude check and make certain that your horizontal relationship with the Body of Christ is all God wants it to be.

God's Measuring Stick

Christianity is more than just a vertical relationship between man on earth and God in heaven. It's also a horizontal relationship between human beings. And the measuring stick God uses to measure the kind of love you have for Him is the love you have for His people.

3

The Unveiling of Jesus Christ

In Philippians 3:10, Paul said, "My desire in life is to know Jesus and to know the power of His resurrection." He added, "I want to be conformed to His sufferings, and, if need be, to experience the same death Jesus died."

That man had a heart for the Lord Jesus Christ! Paul's constant pursuit in life was for an intimate knowing of the Son of God.

Our desire in life should be to know Jesus Christ as He can be known in the power of His Spirit. In order to know Jesus this way, however, each of us must eliminate nonessentials from our life.

What nonessential activities in your life or schedule take from the time you can spend with the Lord? Those activities may be legitimate, but they hinder you from spending time in prayer. They hinder you from spending time in the Word of God. Those are the things we must eliminate if we are to know Jesus in the power and fullness of His Spirit.

Wigglesworth: Man of Prayer

Someone asked Smith Wigglesworth, "How much time do you spend in prayer?"

He replied, "I don't spend more than 15 minutes in prayer, but I never go more than 15 minutes before I pray again." His whole life and schedule were taken up by the Lord Jesus Christ. It's little wonder that he shook continents with the power of God. In fact, it is reported that 22 people were raised from the dead under this man's ministry.

Wigglesworth even raised his wife, Polly, from the dead! She had died at home while he was preaching at a nearby town. Returning home and finding her dead, Wigglesworth called her spirit back into her body. He didn't want her to go. He couldn't bear to lose her.

They talked, and Polly said, "Smith, let me go. I've finished my work here on the Earth." Finally he consented, and she went home to be with Jesus.

When Wigglesworth died at age 87, he did not die with sickness and disease. He was talking to the pastor in a church rectory before the service, and suddenly he exhaled audibly in a long, deep breath, as if in weariness or relief and dropped to the floor. He had finished his ministry here on Earth, so he went home to be with the Lord. What a way to go!

We go because it's time for us to go. We live out the full length of our life determined by God. Then it's our time to be on the other side, so we simply move from planet Earth to heaven. There's glory in that, and that's the kind of home-going I believe God wants for all His people.

Fellowship Lost

As we learned earlier, Jesus Christ addressed seven letters to the churches in Asia Minor—the last one was to the Laodicean church. This letter is the final request He makes of His Church. We don't hear any more from Him in the Scriptures until He comes back for His Church.

What was Jesus' last request? It was a call to intimacy. It was a call to fellowship with Him. Jesus wants our fellowship!

At the beginning, God created the heavens and the Earth. The Garden of Eden was the center of God's creation. On the sixth day, God created man, the crowning glory of His creation. God's original plan for man was fellowship with Him. God created Adam and Eve, and they fellowshipped with Him in the garden in the cool of the day.

Then Adam and Eve violated their relationship with the Lord. They listened to the lies of the serpent and rebelled against the Word of God and brought a curse upon themselves and all their descendants. But God still loved them, even in their fallen condition, so He promised the man and woman that one day the seed of the woman would come and He would completely crush the head of the serpent.

Every prophet of God who spoke by the inspiration of the Holy Spirit, and every sacrifice made by the Levites and the high priests, pointed to a definite moment in time when the Messiah would come.

Almost 2,000 years ago, Jesus Christ, the Son of the living God, the Messiah, the seed of the woman, broke forth across the pages of recorded history.

Jesus lived, ministered, and died the death of the Cross. He was buried and was resurrected on the third day. He ascended to the right hand of God in heaven, where He ever lives to make intercession for the people of God.

Fellowship Restored

Following the death of Jesus Christ, the veil in the Jewish Temple—symbolizing the spiritual separation between God and man—was torn in two from top to bottom. It was God the Father saying to His people, "Come in to Me, and let Me come in to you. I will be to you a Father, and you shall be to Me sons and daughters."

This call to fellowship with God is also seen in John 14, where Jesus said:

> In my Father's house are many mansions: If it were not so, I would have told you. I go to prepare a place for you.
>
> And if I go and prepare a place for you, I will come again, and receive you unto myself; that where I am, there ye may be also.
>
> John 14:2-3

Jesus was speaking prophetically here. He was saying, "I am going to die the death of the Cross. While I am in heaven, I am going to prepare mansions for you. And at an appointed time in history, known only to the Father, I shall return to receive the Church unto Myself."

Right now, Jesus is in heaven, overseeing the construction of our mansions. He is awaiting the command of His Father. In the not too distant future, Jesus will come again and we will be caught up to meet Him in the air.

The Essence of Heaven

The last request Jesus made of His people was for fellowship. He said, "Open the door of your life—open the door of your church—and let Me in. Let's sup together. Let's fellowship together."

Therefore, the very essence of heaven is going to be *fellowship*. Remember, God's original plan for man was to fellowship with him. Fellowship—that's what God longs for. He wants to sit together with you and with me.

The purpose for the human race was that God might have a family, and that He might fellowship with every member of that family.

Christianity is really the story of a father in search of his family. That's what Christianity is all about—God searching out a family that will fellowship with Him.

How To Fellowship With God

Here's the essential question: *How does a person fellowship with the Lord?* There are three answers to that question, and all are correct.

First, through the Word of God. John said that Jesus was the Word of God—he wrote: "And the Word was made flesh, and dwelt among us, (and we beheld his glory, the glory as of the only begotten of the Father), full of grace and truth."

Jesus is the Word of God, and when you meditate in the Scriptures—when you study to show yourself approved unto God—you fellowship with Jesus Christ. The living Word and the written Word are the same. You cannot know Jesus Christ apart from His Word. That's a partial answer.

The second answer is prayer. Prayer is communion and fellowship with Jesus Christ. If you are not consistently praying—if you are not spending time in the presence of God, if you have not built a prayer closet and altar in your home—you cannot know Jesus Christ.

If prayer and the study of God's Word were the only two disciplines necessary to walk in the intimate knowledge of the Son of God, Christianity at best could be practiced in the solitude of a monastery or on the moon.

The third answer is fellowship. Although fellowship may have its origin in the Word of God and in prayer, the practical aspects of the fellowship and the relationship Jesus wants with us always involves other people.

John Defines Fellowship

I've heard people say, "It's just Jesus and me—that's all I need." That's not true. That's only a partial truth. We need each other. In his first epistle, the apostle John describes the relationship and fellowship the disciples had with Jesus during His ministry on Earth:

> That which was from the beginning, which we have heard, which we have seen with our eyes, which we have looked upon, and our hands have handled, of the Word of life;

> (For the life was manifested, and we have seen it, and bear witness, and shew unto you that eternal life, which was with the Father, and was manifested unto us;)
>
> That which we have seen and heard declare we unto you, that ye also may have fellowship with us: and truly our fellowship is with the Father, and with his Son Jesus Christ.
>
> 1 John 1:1-3

Jesus preached to His disciples and the people of ancient Palestine so they could have fellowship with Him, but not with Him alone—so they could have fellowship with each other.

Notice this carefully: God makes no distinction between the fellowship we have with each other and the fellowship we have with Him. There is only one fellowship, and we are all included in that fellowship.

True Fellowship

Let's look at several Scriptures that confirm this. The first is found in Matthew 10:40. Notice what Jesus said here: "He that receiveth you receiveth me . . ." Jesus was saying, "When you receive another Christian, you're receiving Me."

He then continued, "and he that receiveth me receiveth him that sent me." Therefore, when we receive another Christian, not only do we receive Jesus, but we receive the Father as well. On the other hand, if we reject that Christian, who are we rejecting? We're rejecting the Body of Christ—we're rejecting Jesus Himself. And if we reject Jesus, we're rejecting the Father as well.

Every Christian is part of the fellowship God has ordained for us, and we have no recourse but to receive them and love them.

Loving the Unlovely

Some people are rather easy to love, but others can be challenging at times. Nonetheless, we need each one. In fact, we may need the most challenging person more than we do the most amiable person, because the challenging person is going to develop in us patience and long-suffering, qualities that are the fruit of the Spirit.

Apart from the fruit of the Spirit developing in our lives through fellowship, we cannot fully know Jesus Christ—because Jesus is the personification of all the fruit of the Spirit.

4

Healing Broken Relationships

> Therefore if thou bring thy gift to the altar, and there rememberest that thy brother hath ought against thee;
>
> Leave there thy gift before the altar, and go thy way; first be reconciled to thy brother, and then come and offer thy gift.
>
> Matthew 5:23-24

Jesus placed a great deal of emphasis on relationships. In effect, He said, "If you have a gift in hand, and you go to the altar to give that gift to the Lord, and while there you remember a brother who has something against you, set your gift aside, find that person, and be reconciled.

"Let the love of God heal that relationship, and then return to the altar and give that gift to God. For then and only then shall I find satisfaction and meaning in your gift. If your relationship with your brother or your sister is broken, your relationship with Me is broken, and the gift means nothing."

The Lord Jesus Christ cannot have the kind of fellowship with us He wants to have as long as our fellowship with another believer has been broken. Why? Christ has identified Himself in that person, so if our relationship with them has been broken, our friendship with Christ has been broken as well.

Christians, therefore, must love each other. If there's something in your heart or mine that's not right toward another Christian and it's taking away from the kind of relationship God wants us to have with them, we're under divine obligation to seek out that person and find a place of healing.

As we saw, Christian brothers and sisters who receive us are receiving Jesus; and when we receive them, it means we're receiving Jesus. When we reject our brothers and sisters, however, we're rejecting a part of Jesus, because they are bone of His bone and flesh of His flesh and filled with His Spirit—no matter how ugly their attitude.

Every Evil Work

James says strife leads to every evil work: "For where envying and strife is, there is confusion and every evil work" (James 3:16).

If you're having a problem with someone, work it out with that person. Don't leave his or her presence until peace and love are flowing between you, because where there's a chink in our unity, the enemy can come in and take us captive. God hates strife with a holy anger, because when we refuse to accept one another, when we are unkind to one another, or when we defame each other, we injure the Lord Jesus Christ Himself. We are refusing bone of His bone and flesh of His flesh—those whose fellowship He has ordained for our lives.

When you made Jesus your Lord and Savior, God deposited something of Himself in you—something of Himself that is important to other Christians. You are a certain facet of Jesus, and they cannot know Him fully without receiving you. And you cannot know Him fully without receiving them.

Receiving Jesus in Others

In Matthew 25, we find what Jesus says about receiving Him when we receive others.

> Then shall the King say unto them on his right hand, Come, ye blessed of my Father, inherit the kingdom prepared for you from the foundation of the world:
>
> For I was an hungred, and ye gave me meat: I was thirsty, and ye gave me drink: I was a stranger, and ye took me in:
>
> Naked, and ye clothed me: I was sick, and ye visited me: I was in prison, and ye came unto me.
>
> Then shall the righteous answer him, saying, Lord, when saw we thee an hungred, and fed thee? or thirsty, and gave thee drink?
>
> When saw we thee a stranger, and took thee in? or naked, and clothed thee?
>
> Or when saw we thee sick, or in prison, and came unto thee?
>
> Matthew 25:34-39

I can see a smile on Jesus' face right now. He's about to tell them.

> And the King shall answer and say unto them, Verily I say unto you, Inasmuch as ye have done it unto one of the least of these my brethren, ye have done it unto me.
>
> Matthew 25:40

These people were ministering to each other, caring for each other, loving each other, and helping each other.

Jesus, in essence, said, "When you do it to each other, you do it to Me, because you are each bone of My bone and flesh of My flesh. You can't separate the Head from the Body, because whatever you do for My people, I am in the middle of the transaction and I am receiving ministry."

But what happens if we don't help each other? Look at what Jesus said about the consequences of that:

> Then shall he say also unto them on the left hand, Depart from me, ye cursed, into everlasting fire, prepared for the devil and his angels:
>
> For I was an hungred, and ye gave me no meat: I was thirsty, and ye gave me no drink:
>
> I was a stranger, and ye took me not in: naked, and ye clothed me not: sick, and in prison, and ye visited me not.
>
> Then shall they also answer him, saying, Lord, when saw we thee an hungred, or athirst, or a

> stranger, or naked, or sick, or in prison, and did not minister unto thee?
>
> Then shall he answer them, saying, Verily I say unto you, Inasmuch as ye did it not to one of the least of these, ye did it not to me.
>
> And these shall go away into everlasting punishment: but the righteous into life eternal.
>
> Matthew 25:41-46

Kingdom Greatness

These are strong words—words that we should take to heart so we don't neglect doing what Jesus said.

Another example of helping each other is found in Mark 9:

> And he came to Capernaum: and being in the house he asked them, What was it that ye disputed among yourselves by the way?
>
> But they held their peace: for by the way they had disputed among themselves, who should be the greatest.
>
> And he sat down, and called the twelve, and saith unto them, If any man desire to be first, the same shall be last of all, and servant of all.
>
> Mark 9:33-35

If you want to be great in the kingdom of God, you must take a towel, wrap it around yourself, and wash people's feet. That's the definition of kingdom greatness.

Receiving a Child

Notice what Jesus said next:

> And he took a child, and set him in the midst of them: and when he had taken him in his arms, he said unto them,
>
> Whosoever shall receive one of such children in my name, receiveth me: and whosoever shall receive me, receiveth not me, but him that sent me.
>
> Mark 9:36-37

In our society there's a phrase: "throwaway children." We've all heard it. Our society also says, "Children have no rights." That's not what Jesus said.

Jesus took a child "and set him in the midst of them." What do you suppose this said to His disciples? What is it saying to you and me?

Jesus said, "If you receive this child, this little one, you receive Me—and not just Me, but the One who sent Me." What did the Lord mean by saying this? He was saying, "If you are to experience a genuine love exchange with God, if you are to experience a genuine love exchange with Me, that love exchange will manifest itself in the attitude and relationship you have with other people. If you won't receive them, you aren't receiving Me."

A Part of Jesus

Look around the congregation the next time you go to church. What do you see? Well, there's old

John, and there's Susan, Paul, and Debbie. No, they're much more than those names, much more than the bodies you see. They're bone of His bone and flesh of His flesh. They're a part of Jesus!

The Head of the Church has a Body, just like your head has a body. And every person in your congregation is a part of Jesus. They are a part of the fellowship that God has ordained for your life, and you need them. *You need them!*

As we progress through this book, you'll understand why you need them. The person you're being mean to, the person you're not communicating with, the person you're not receiving, is the person you need the most! And until you heal that relationship, you keep Jesus Christ standing at the door of your life.

He'll stand out there knocking and saying, "Let Me in," because that's His nature. He never gives up on us. He is married to the backslider and the lukewarm. And He is coming for His Church—but first He is going to make her "holy and without blemish" (Ephesians 5:27).

5

The New Commandment

The apostle Paul wrote more about the Body of Christ than any other New Testament writer. He used the human body as a metaphor to describe the spiritual Body of Christ.

> And Saul, yet breathing out threatenings and slaughter [NKJV: murder] against the disciples of the Lord, went unto the high priest,
>
> And desired of him letters to Damascus to the synagogues, that if he found any of this way, whether they were men or women, he might bring them bound unto Jerusalem.
>
> And as he journeyed, he came near Damascus: and suddenly there shined round about him a light from heaven:
>
> And he fell to the earth, and heard a voice saying unto him, Saul, Saul, why persecutest thou me?
>
> And he said, Who art thou, Lord? And the Lord said, I am Jesus whom thou persecutest: it is hard for thee to kick against the pricks.

> And he trembling and astonished said, Lord, what wilt thou have me do?
>
> Acts 9:1-6

We have no historical or biblical record of Saul's ever having encountered Jesus in the flesh. Yet Jesus said, "Saul, you are persecuting Me. You have lifted your hand against Me."

Head and Body: Indivisible

Who was Paul persecuting? He was persecuting the Church. Who is the Church? The Church is the Body of Christ, and the Head cannot be separated from the Body.

If Jesus were to appear in our midst today, would we see His head alone, or would we see His body as well? We would see the whole person, wouldn't we? In the same way, you cannot separate the spiritual Body of Christ from the headship of Jesus Christ. They are joined together.

Therefore, when someone persecutes a member of the Body—when another saint (or a sinner) is unkind to you, hurts you, or seeks to injure you—Jesus says to them, "You're hurting Me. You've lifted your hand against the bone of My bone and flesh of My flesh—My Body!"

Paul's Sufferings

When you think about the life of Paul, you can't help but remember the tremendous sacrifices he made for the people of God.

Paul suffered much for the Lord Jesus Christ and for His Church. His credentials as an apostle were the things he suffered for the Body of Christ and for people everywhere. He understood perfectly the principle the Lord taught him: the Head cannot be separated from the Body.

Likewise, we cannot separate each other from Jesus. Jesus makes no distinction between the kind of fellowship we have with Him and the kind of fellowship we have with each other.

When we receive each other, we receive Jesus. When we turn each other away, we turn Jesus away. When we're unkind to each other, we're unkind to Jesus.

If I say, for example, "I don't like Joe Christian," I'm saying I don't like Jesus, because Joe Christian is bone of His bone and flesh of His flesh.

God has ordained Joe for my life, and there is something about the man that reveals Jesus to me. Apart from knowing and receiving Joe, I cannot know that part of Jesus. There is something of Jesus in Joe, just as there is something of Jesus in you, and there is something of Jesus in me. That's why Christians need each other. Collectively, we are His Body.

> Then they that gladly received his word were baptized: and the same day there were added unto them about three thousand souls.
> Acts 2:41

Four Disciplines

In Acts 4:42, four disciplines are mentioned: "And they continued steadfastly in the apostles' doctrine and fellowship, and in breaking of bread, and in prayers." The four disciplines in this verse are: (1) doctrine, (2) fellowship, (3) breaking of bread, and (4) prayers.

The passage continues:

> And fear [or awe of God] came upon every soul: and many wonders and signs were done by the apostles.
>
> And all that believed were together, and had all things common;
>
> And sold their possessions and goods, and parted them to all men, as every man had need.
>
> And they, continuing daily with one accord in the temple, and breaking bread from house to house, did eat their meat with gladness and singleness of heart,
>
> Praising God, and having favour with all the people. And the Lord added to the church daily such as should be saved.
>
> Acts 2:43-47

Notice that two of the four disciplines in verse 42 are directed toward God—they identify the vertical relationship we have with Jesus. The remaining two disciplines are directed toward man—they identify the horizontal relationships we have with each other.

There are "Lone Rangers" in the Body of Christ—God's hermits. They usually hide out in front of a television set, saying, "That's church." But God has called us to be *spiritually and physically* together.

I realize, of course, there are people who are disabled in some way and can't make it to the house of God. In those cases, thank God for Christian television—it meets a large part of their needs. But they still need Christians to visit them and fellowship with them.

A Dynamic Is Released When We Meet Together

When we have strength in our body, we can join ourselves to and with the Body of Christ. We have no business remaining at home. We need each other.

Something happens in the house of God. A dynamic is released to work in us that reveals Jesus Christ. It happens in the sanctuary. It happens in Sunday School. It happens through small group ministry. It happens as we gather together.

What do we learn in the Word, and what do we learn in prayer? We learn about Jesus. Everything we learn vertically, we are to practice horizontally. What we learn vertically has no meaning if we don't practice it by ministering to one another—if we do not give our lives for one another.

What makes these passages from the Book of Acts so powerful is this: the Lord added to the Church daily those that should be saved. Who were being saved? The same people who had crucified Christ just weeks before.

Irresistible Love

These people saw something at work in the early Church. They saw the love of God at work in those believers. And what they saw was irresistible. What they saw spoke volumes to them. They saw people giving their lives for each other. What they saw said to them, "Jesus is alive."

The believers prayed and sought the Lord through the Word. What they learned about Jesus, they put into practice in fellowship.

In that discipline of fellowship, they broke bread with each other, and Jesus became a real person to them—a person they began to exhibit to one another. When the city saw Jesus in His believers' lives, they came to Him in droves.

Witnesses to Jesus' Resurrection

As people of God, we have the same two witnesses that tell the world Jesus is alive.

The first is miracles, signs, and wonders.

The second is the love we have for each other.

In the thirteenth chapter of John it tells how at the Last Supper Jesus wrapped a towel around Himself, took a basin of water, and washed the feet of His disciples. He washed Peter's feet, John's feet, and even Judas' feet:

> So after he had washed their feet, and had taken his garments, and was set down again, he said unto them, Know ye what I have done to you?
>
> Ye call me Master and Lord: and ye say well; for so I am.
>
> If I then, your Lord and Master, have washed your feet; ye also ought to wash one another's feet.
>
> For I have given you an example, that ye should do as I have done to you.
>
> John 13:12-15

The kind of attitude Jesus wants us to have toward each other can be seen in this passage. What attitude did He have toward Judas? He loved Judas. He didn't want

Judas to perish, even though Judas was the Benedict Arnold of his day. Judas committed high treason against the Son of God by choosing to sell his loyalty and relationship with Jesus for 30 pieces of silver.

The Servant Is Not Greater

Jesus said further:

> Verily, verily, I say to you, The servant is not greater than his lord; neither he that is sent greater than he that sent him.
>
> If ye know these things, happy are ye if ye do them.
>
> John 13:16-17

There is joy that comes to the servant of God that the world cannot understand. There is joy associated with humility. There is joy that comes as we love those who persecute us and speak all manner of evil against us.

We must know these things. We need revelation. We should ask, "God, what are You saying to me in this? What have You hidden in these Scriptures? Lord, whatever You have locked away in these Scriptures, reveal it to me so I can be a doer of the Word, not just a hearer only.

"Lord, You are saying here that there is a joy that comes with service. You are saying that the greatest in the kingdom of God will be the servant of all—he is going to be the person who washes feet."

A New Commandment

Chapter 13 of John ends dramatically with Jesus saying:

> A new commandment I give unto you, That ye love one another; as I have loved you, that ye also love one another.
> By this shall all men know that ye are my disciples, if ye have love one to another.
> John 13:34-35

"A new commandment I give unto you." He gave them a new commandment to add to the two great commandments He had already told them about:

> Then one of them, which was a lawyer, asked him a question, tempting him, and saying,
> Master, which is the great commandment in the law?
> Jesus said unto him, Thou shalt love the Lord thy God with all thy heart, and with all thy soul, and with all thy mind.
> This is the first and great commandment.
> And the second is like unto it, Thou shalt love thy neighbour as thyself.
> On these two commandments hang all the law and the prophets.
> Matthew 22:35-40

Jesus said, "I am giving you a new commandment." What is it? Are you ready for this? It's about love again: "That ye love one another; as I have loved you." That's the new commandment. You are not only to love God and your neighbor, but every Christian just as Jesus loves you—and Jesus gave His life for you!

"That's a mighty tall order."

I didn't write the Bible.

"I love Jesus, but I'm still working on loving our pastor."

I didn't write the Bible.

Our primary witness to a lost and dying world is when we love one another. Do you know what this kind of love does? It manifests Jesus in us.

The True Child of God

The Lord, in effect, was saying here, "The distinguishing mark of every true child of God will be *agape* love" (see 1 John 3:14).

The children of Israel didn't really understand *agape* love. They believed God was a big guy sitting in the sky, and if they were to step out of line, He would squash them like a bug. That was the picture most of them had of God. God was going to get them if they didn't watch out!

When Jesus came to Earth, He introduced a new kind of love—*agape* love—a divine kind of love, a supernatural kind of love, a love that always prefers the other person, a love that always sees the other person as valuable and precious. The love of God never hurts people—it always benefits them.

Time Doesn't Always Heal

Maybe someone hurt you, and you've carried the pain around in your heart for a long time. There's a saying, "Time heals all wounds," but that isn't necessarily true.

Yes, the more time that elapses after the conflict, the more likely you are to forget the fullness of the pain you felt in that moment, but only forgiveness heals all wounds.

If you are out of sorts with another member of the Body of Christ, go to that person and heal the relationship. Remember, if your relationship with another Christian is broken, your relationship with the Lord is broken as well.

Regardless of who was the source of the conflict—whether it was you or the other person—you're under divine obligation to go to the person who has wronged you, violated you, spoken evil of you, or worked to undermine your integrity, and seek to resolve every conflict that may exist between you, restoring your relationship.

To do so is a real mark of maturity. To refuse to do so is an evidence of immaturity. If the person accepts you, you have gained a brother or sister.

When I have taught on this subject, people have come to me after the service and said, "When you said that, suddenly I was reminded of a relationship that fell apart years ago and was never resolved. I can still feel the pain of it, and I know I need to bring healing to it." One person said, "I'm going to find my brother and restore our relationship."

That's what you need to do. Don't shovel dirt over your broken relationship, bury it, and pretend it never happened. Heal it. Do everything you can to be freed from it. If you don't, you're keeping something alive that needs to die.

Trust Jesus With the Results

"What if I'm not received by the other person?"

If the other person rejects you, that's between God and them. You've done what God required of you, and you'll be able to walk away from the situation knowing you tried. From that point on, all you can do is pray for the person and trust Jesus with the results.

Paul, inspired by the Holy Spirit, wrote that because such people had not discerned the Body of Christ, they suffered the consequences. "For this cause many are weak and sickly among you, and many sleep [have died]."

The passage continues, "For if we would judge ourselves, we should not be judged. But when we are judged, we are chastened of the Lord, that we should not be condemned with the world" (see 1 Corinthians 11:29-32).

Jesus said, in essence, "If you come to the altar with a gift for God and while there remember a brother who has something against you, take the gift, set it aside, and go find your brother. Be reconciled with your brother. Restore that relationship.

"Let the Body of Christ be one, not divided and broken, but whole. Once you've done that, come back, take up the gift, and give it to God, for then and only then will the gift mean something."

We're so eager to give gifts, yet we've left a trail of 'dead bodies' in our wake.

But our Lord tells us that He doesn't want us to bring Him broken relationships. He wants healing, restoration, friendship, relationship, fellowship, and love.

When you turn to pick people up and heal them, then you can come to the Lord with your gift. It will make the Lord happy, and you can smile again.

6

The Benefits of Fellowship

Thus far we have emphasized our responsibilities concerning fellowship. Now let's examine the privileges of fellowship.

What do you think the responses would be if I were to ask Christians the following two questions:

"If the Lord wanted to edify you, how would He do it?"

"If the Lord wanted to encourage and strengthen you, how would He do that?"

No doubt someone would reply, "Well, I would go to the Word of God. The Lord would speak to me from His Word." We've all had the Lord do that for us. "Then I would go to the Lord in prayer, and while I was in prayer, the Lord would encourage me. I would sense His presence." And that, too, has happened to each of us.

But those are the exceptions to the rule, not the normal way. *God usually uses people to edify and encourage us.* Here are examples of the majority of answers I've received in response to those questions when I've asked them in meetings.

"I was sick in body, and I asked the pastor to lay hands on me. The power of God went through me, and the Lord delivered me."

"I was in need—our cupboards were bare—and I didn't know what we were going to do. All of a sudden, there was a knock at the door. There stood some friends from our church who had brought bags of groceries to us. It was the Lord meeting our need through them."

"I was discouraged. I was being oppressed of the enemy. Then a sister and a brother from my church called me on the telephone, saying, 'The Lord has put you on my heart, and I just want to have a word of prayer with you.'"

The primary way God chooses to meet needs in the Body of Christ is through other people, because each of us is bone of His bone and flesh of His flesh.

Becoming Christ for Someone Else

A woman in our church shared a wonderful testimony in one service. For days, her younger brother was on her heart. She would say to her mother, "Mom, I've got my brother on my heart," and her mother would reply, "Oh, Mary, he's doing fine."

But he wasn't doing fine. In fact, this young man was contemplating suicide. He had lost hope. One night he loaded a revolver and was holding it, preparing to take his life. In desperation he looked toward heaven and prayed, "Jesus, if You're really there, and You really love me, help me!"

At that moment, Mary responded to a sudden increase of compassion from the Lord and picked up the telephone and called her brother.

With one hand still holding the revolver, he reached for the phone and picked it up.

Mary said, "Honey, I just want you to know that Jesus has put you on my heart, and I've been praying for you."

The young man put the gun down and received the love of God through his sister. Mary became Jesus Christ to him—bone of His bone and flesh of His flesh—reaching out to bless and help him. This is the kind of maturity God is looking for in His people.

Paul Is Comforted

Wearied from his journeys, the apostle Paul was comforted by a visit from Titus as he recorded in 2 Corinthians 7:

> For, when we were come into Macedonia, our flesh had no rest, but we were troubled on every side; without were fightings, within were fears.
>
> Nevertheless God, that comforteth those that are cast down, comforted us by the coming of Titus;
>
> And not by his coming only, but by the consolation wherewith he was comforted in you, when he told us your earnest desire, your mourning, your fervent mind toward me; so that I rejoiced the more.
>
> 2 Corinthians 7:5-7

Do you have the picture? Here's Paul, his flesh having no rest, troubled on every side. Without were fightings—within were fears. Paul was in a dark place. He needed encouragement, and the Lord sent Titus to him.

THE REVELATION OF JESUS

Prior to his coming to be with Paul, Titus had spent time with the Corinthians, and they had ministered to him. He shared with Paul the encouragement they had given him.

Do you know what Titus was to Paul? He was the hands of Jesus Christ reaching out for Paul.

Do you know who the Corinthian Christians were? They were Jesus Christ—bone of His bone and flesh of His flesh—reaching out to bless another member in the Body of Christ.

Whenever you reach out to help or bless another Christian, the Lord is in the midst of that ministry. It's not just you—it's Jesus Christ Himself coming to that person.

Ananias Obeys

> And there was a certain disciple at Damascus, named Ananias; and to him said the Lord in a vision, Ananias. And he said, Behold, I am here, Lord.
>
> And the Lord said unto him, Arise, and go into the street which is called Straight, and inquire in the house of Judas for one called Saul, of Tarsus: for, behold, he prayeth.
>
> And hath seen in a vision a man named Ananias coming in, and putting his hand on him, that he might receive his sight.
>
> Acts 9:10-12

Although the Lord spoke to Ananias while he was in prayer and told him to go lay hands on Saul of Tarsus so he might receive his sight, Ananias wasn't overjoyed about going and replied:

> Then Ananias answered, Lord, I have heard by many of this man, how much evil he hath done to thy saints at Jerusalem:
> And here he hath authority from the chief priests to bind all that call on thy name.
> But the Lord said unto him, Go thy way: for he is a chosen vessel unto me, to bear my name before the Gentiles, and kings, and the children of Israel.
> Acts 9:13-15

Urged by the Lord, Ananias obeyed, and when he reached Saul (later Paul) he said, "Brother Saul, the Lord, even Jesus, . . . hath sent me, that thou mightest receive thy sight, and be filled with the Holy Ghost" (Acts 9:17).

When Ananias laid his hands on Saul, scales fell from his eyes and they were healed, and he received the Holy Spirit.

Who Was Ananias?

Ananias was Jesus to Paul! He was the Lord's hands to Paul. It wasn't Ananias' hands that were placed upon Paul; it was the hands of Jesus Christ that touched him that day.

Do you know what the Lord was saying to Ananias? He was saying, in effect, "Ananias, if you don't go, I can't go. If you don't lay your hands on Saul, I can't lay My hands on him. Ananias, don't you understand that you are bone of My bone and flesh of My flesh? When you reach out to touch Saul, I reach out to touch Saul."

Making Excuses

Has God ever said to you in prayer, "I want you to call this person. I want you to go to your neighbor's house. I want you to witness to the people who live on your block."

We've made excuses. "Lord, I can't knock on doors. I can't pass out tracts. The people won't receive me."

Yet in all of this, the Lord was saying, "If you don't go, I can't go. If you won't witness, I can't witness. If you don't make that telephone call, I can't make that telephone call."

Jesus does nothing apart from His people.

He has not called angels to spread the Gospel and fulfill the Great Commission. He has called people like you and me to share the Gospel with the people living in our community. This means that if Satan can silence us, he can silence the voice of God in every city.

When we truly comprehend this, we will recognize how essential we are, not just to the Body of Christ, but to all those where we live who don't know Jesus Christ as their Lord and Savior.

Someday in your church, look around the congregation and catch someone's eye and say, "Jesus, I love You!"

Grab that person by the hand and say, "You are bone of my bone and flesh of my flesh. The same Spirit that dwells in you dwells in me. We are one. When I pray for you, I pray for myself. When I pray for you, I pray for Jesus Christ. Jesus, I love You!"

7

Visions of Jesus

I've been a Christian for 27 years, and during those years I've seen Jesus on two occasions.

The first occasion was almost 20 years ago. A good friend of mine, Dick Mills, gave me a prophetic word about a vision that I would have in the night that would be an appearance of Jesus. Several months later it took place just as he said it would.

When I saw Jesus that first time, He said nothing. He didn't need to. I fully understood the significance of the vision. I saw the living Christ, and He was the written Word.

A few years ago, the Lord appeared to me a second time. In this second vision, I heard Jesus speak, and what He said crushed me. I became a broken man. I wept uncontrollably over the words I heard the Lord speak. I am going to share that vision with you at the end of this chapter.

Whenever Jesus Christ appears to you, it's significant. It's not like Jesus doesn't have better things to do. He doesn't suddenly announce to His angels, "I don't have anything to do today, so I think I'll appear to Jill Christian." The Lord doesn't work that way. He is exact in everything He does.

An Image of the Apostle John

The apostle John, one of the Lord's disciples, referred to himself as that disciple whom the Lord loves. Whenever I think of John, I always think of the Last Supper.

Perhaps you have a different image of John. Perhaps you think of him as being one of the "sons of thunder," and there have been times when you, like John, wanted to call fire down from heaven on people (Luke 9:54).

But that's not the mental picture I have of John. I see John at the Last Supper. He was the disciple who sat next to Jesus and lay his head on Jesus' chest. He felt the warmth emanating from Jesus. Think of that!

He could hear the very heartbeat of the Son of God as His heart pumped blood through His veins. John loved Jesus with all his heart.

John wrote five of the books we have in the Bible: The Gospel of John; the three epistles—First, Second, and Third John; and the Book of Revelation. John had more to say about the love of God than any other writer in the New Testament.

John's Vision of Jesus

At one point in his life, John was banished to a life in prison, a life of solitude, on the island of Patmos. But Jesus can find you no matter where you are. He can come to you in your darkest hour when you feel as if there is no person on the face of the Earth who really cares about you.

Jesus came to John on Patmos, and John saw the resurrected, glorified Christ in all His majesty and splendor. He saw Jesus' eyes as flames of fire. He saw Jesus' face shining as the sun in all of its strength. He saw His hair, white as wool; His feet as fine brass, refined in a furnace. He saw a two-edged sword coming out of His mouth. He heard His voice as the sound of many waters.

When John saw and heard Jesus, he was so frightened, so overwhelmed by the glorified Christ, he fell as a dead man at His feet. The Lord stood him upright and said, "Don't be afraid." Then Jesus gave him letters to the seven churches in Asia Minor.

Jesus' Sacrifice of Love

Some verses in 1 John 4 have meant a great deal to me through the years. For example, John says in verse 19, "We love him, [why?] because he first loved us." Jesus loved us when we were unlovable. Jesus died for us while we were yet sinners. He was the Lamb slain from the foundation of the world.

Years ago I heard someone say, "It wasn't nails holding Jesus on the Cross; it was love—His love for you and me—that kept Him there."

Jesus had the power to free Himself (Matthew 26:53), yet He died the death of the Cross as our substitute because of His love for us. And because He loves us, we love Him also. We are returning to Him the love He has put in our hearts.

Then John writes:

> If a man say, I love God, and hateth his brother, he is a liar: for he that loveth not his brother whom he hath seen, how can he love God whom he hath not seen?
>
> And this commandment have we from him, That he who loveth God love his brother also.
>
> 1 John 4:20-21

Divine Obligation To Love

If you say, "I love God," you are then under divine obligation to love your Christian brother and sister as well.

Do you know how impractical we have been through the years? We like to talk about our love for a God whom we cannot see, while we refuse to love people whom we can see.

The yardstick—the measuring rod God uses to measure the kind of love you have for Him—is the love you have for your brother and sister in Christ.

If you say to the Lord, "Lord, I love You; it's Bob I don't like," this is what the Lord hears: "Because I don't like Bob, I don't like You." But your friend Bob is a member of Christ's Body. Ephesians 5:30 says we are members of His Body, of His flesh, and of His bones. And the Head cannot be separated from the Body.

What if Bob appeared in the sanctuary some Sunday morning as a head rolling down the aisle? You would be alarmed at the sight. "There goes Bob's head," someone would say. "What's wrong with Bob? Where's his body?"

But if Bob came in complete with head, torso, arms, legs, and feet, you would think nothing of it. You wouldn't be concerned at all because that's the natural and normal way of things—the head and body always go together.

Check Your Attitude

The attitude we take toward the Body is the attitude we have toward Jesus Christ Himself.

All of us like the expressive parts of the Body of Christ: the hands, the eyes, and the tongue. They're exciting. And all of us enjoy being around lovely people. We like people who are good-looking, dress well, and always have a smile and a kind word.

But lovely people don't challenge our ability to love. They don't initiate growth in our life—it's the uncomely parts of the Body of Christ who do that. Even though we don't think these uncomely parts are important to our lives, they are essential to us.

When we must use our faith—when we must grow up and keep our heart attitude right to love the uncomely parts—it produces growth in our lives.

Have you ever met someone who rubbed your fur the wrong way? We've all known Christians who walk through life with a chip on their shoulder. It doesn't take much to get them into trouble with the Body of Christ; they're willing to fight at the drop of a hat. They're probably one of those uncomely parts we need.

Have you ever had a cat whose fur you rubbed the wrong way? It felt uncomfortable to both you and the cat.

So stroke the fur the right way. That's the attitude we need to take toward the uncomely parts of the Body of Christ.

The Family of God

The people who sit next to you, in front of you, and behind you in church are not only members of the family of God, they are necessary to you.

In some of my services, I invite people to look at the person sitting next to them, smile, take their hand, and squeeze their hand tenderly—letting them know they're happy they're sitting next to them, and they really do care about them.

I ask them to look at each other and say, "You're necessary to me. You're the key to my being developed in the love of God. You're the key to my knowing Jesus. Without you, I can only know about Him, but with you I can *know* Him.

"Together we are bone of His bone and flesh of His flesh. We are members of His Body. I can see Jesus in you. In fact, you are Jesus to me."

Making God Visible

In 1 John 4:11, John said, "Beloved, if God so loved us . . ." Here's the question: Does God love us? Next, John tells us what our response should be to that question: "we ought also to love one another."

Then John said something that has absolutely changed my life:

> No man hath seen God at any time. If we love one another, God dwelleth in us, and his love is perfected in us.
>
> 1 John 4:12

There are two thoughts in that verse. First, the way we make the invisible God visible to a lost and dying world is by loving each other.

Do you remember that Jesus said in John 13:34-35, "I am giving you a new commandment." They had the two great commandments—to love God and to love their neighbor. But Jesus said, in effect, "I am adding to those a new commandment: I want you to love each other just as I love you." He went on to say, "By this kind of love—by *agape* love—all men are going to know that you are My disciples."

He was saying that the way we make Christ visible to people who cannot see Him is through our loving one another.

Can you imagine what the world thinks of the Church and God when they see churches in strife and splitting, and Christians arguing with each other? It has the opposite effect.

I've heard testimonies like this and so have you: "I wouldn't go to that church. They're just a bunch of hypocrites. They talk about God, but they don't live godly. They talk like they're Christians but they don't act like Christians are supposed to."

Why Children Rebel

Yes, we are a people under construction, and no one knows better than you and I that we are not finished products. We've all said and done a lot of things through the years that we shouldn't have.

For example, we want to gossip, and the Holy Spirit tries to stop us, but we override His voice and say it anyway. We didn't have to say it—God tried to stop us—but we chose to do it.

Because of our actions, many will not come to Christ. Because of our actions, there are children who are living in rebellion today. They saw their parents get hurt by Christians, and they said, "I don't want to have anything to do with Christianity."

Let's look at the text again:

> No man hath seen God at any time. If we love one another, God dwelleth in us, and his love is perfected in us.
>
> 1 John 4:12

The second thought in this verse is, "If we love one another. . . " Stop! Do you see that? Read it again: "If we love one another, God dwelleth in us, and his love is perfected in us."

Perfected in God's Love

If we love one another, God's love is perfected in us. How is His love perfected in us? By our loving one another. We cannot be perfected in the love of God apart from loving each other.

In other words, other Christians are my key to being developed in the love of God, and I am their key to being developed in the love of God. So we're not just family—we're all necessary to each other.

I cannot be perfected or developed in the love of God apart from having a relationship with other Christians. Why is it so necessary that we develop in love? Who is love? God is love!

Love is not a feeling or an emotion. Love can produce emotions and feelings, but love is much deeper than a feeling, a few tears, or a few goose bumps.

God is love. Jesus is Emmanuel, God with us. He is Emmanuel, love with us.

Apart from our being perfected or developed in the love of God, we can have no real revelation of the character and nature of God, because He is love.

Operating in Love

How can we know Him who is love unless we are operating in love? And how can we operate in the love of God if we walk through life slandering people?

There are a lot of people throughout the world who know about God. They will pull out their "Gospel guns" and shoot you down in a second with their doctrine. They will say, "You don't believe the way I do, and you're wrong—bang, bang, bang!"

Yes, they know about God, but love doesn't act that way, and Jesus wouldn't treat people that way. Jesus is big enough to take care of such people. Just stop complaining and start praying. In time the Lord will straighten out everyone's doctrine—including mine.

The Bible says we prophesy in part and we know in part. This means there is another part we don't know. This means, no one knows everything in this life.

My Doctrine Changes

My doctrine has changed through the years. The first church I belonged to was the Southern Baptist Church. I signed the church rolls because my mother went to church there.

My wife, Shelvia, was raised in a tongue-talking, Spirit-baptized, Pentecostal preacher's home. Her earliest recollection of church was of sleeping under a pew during the services when she was a little girl.

In those days, Pentecostal women didn't cut their hair, and when they danced in the Spirit, the hairpins would fall out of their hairdos, and their hair would fall down and fly about their heads. That was church.

I remember the first service Shelvia and I ever attended in that Southern Baptist Church. Somehow the pastor learned that we were hanging out with that "tongue-talking crowd." When he saw us come through the doors, he changed his entire message and preached against the baptism in the Holy Spirit. That was okay, it was part of the Lord's way of training us to walk in love with those who disagreed with our doctrines.

Learning From the Body of Christ

I have found through the years that you can learn things from the entire Body of Christ. In the Southern Baptist Church I learned how to win people for God.

The moment you segregate yourself—the moment you cut yourself off from the rest of the Body of Christ—you stop growing. You stop learning truths that can bless you and other people.

One of the greatest Presbyterian theologians that a denomination ever produced once said, "I had an opportunity to stop off in Springfield, Missouri, and I visited with some of the brethren from another denomination."

I knew the organization he was referring to—it was the Assemblies of God. (I had credentials with them for many years.) The Presbyterian theologian continued, "We sat together and spoke about Jesus. To my surprise, I learned that we only differed in three percent of our doctrine. The common denominator we had as fellow members in the Church was our mutual love for Jesus Christ and the faith we had in Him."

When I heard him say that, it spoke volumes to my life. I thought, "Here the Church has been majoring in the minors! We have allowed three percent of our doctrine to divide us. We have said, 'Don't go over there and talk to those Southern Baptists. Don't talk to those Pentecostals. Don't talk to those Mennonites.'"

We've allowed three percent of our doctrine to bring division, instead of allowing the 97 percent to bring harmony.

A "Jesus Christ Heaven"

God has a big family. It's not going to be a Presbyterian heaven. It's not going to be a Pentecostal heaven. It's going to be a Jesus Christ heaven!

And every man, woman, teenager, boy, and girl bought by the blood of the Lamb, cleansed by the blood of the Lamb, is going to make heaven their home one day. It took me a long time to grow enough to be able to say that.

Other Christians like you are the key to my being developed in the love of God. They are the key to my really knowing Jesus Christ intimately.

The Word alone is not enough. Prayer alone is not enough. We can study until our eyeballs fall out. We can pray until our hair falls out. We can be full of knowledge, but what are we going to do with that knowledge? That knowledge should be shared—not only with sinners but also with saints.

As we learned earlier, Christianity is much more than just a vertical relationship, it's a horizontal relationship as well. Everything we learn about God in the vertical relationship, we practice on each other in the horizontal relationship.

In the process, we come to know Jesus Christ intimately—*intimately*. Like John of old, we will learn to hear the very heartbeat of the Son of God. We'll feel warmth radiating from Him.

My Second Vision of Jesus

Now let me share about the second vision God gave me. It proved to be one of the most powerful, life-changing encounters I've ever had with Jesus Christ. When the truth in 1 John 4:12—which says that loving people is the key to being perfected in the love of God—broke across my spirit, I suddenly found myself in the Spirit, and Jesus appeared to me.

I could see Jesus clearly, but I also could see people—some black, some white, some brown, some yellow, some red. I could see the color of their eyes—blue, hazel, brown, black, green, etc.

They were living figures. I could see their clothing, yet there was a transparency about them. I could see through them. It was as if they were crystalline figures.

Standing on the other side of these people was the Lord Jesus Christ. His arms were outstretched to me. He called me by name, saying, "Tom, will you come love Me? Tom, will you come serve Me?"

Getting to Jesus Through You

As I looked at Him, I was struck with the realization that I could not love Jesus apart from loving the people that were between us. And to reach Him, I would have to go through them.

Suddenly I realized that I could not serve Jesus apart from serving His people. But who are they, who are you? Bone of His bone and flesh of His flesh, filled with His Spirit, created in His likeness and His image.

I realized that my loving and serving others translated into my loving and serving Jesus Christ, the Head of the Church. The Head and the Body cannot be separated—they are one.

My Heart Breaks

Do you know what emotions I felt following that experience? I was crushed. Crushed! My heart was broken. I wept uncontrollably, convulsively, before God over the fact that I had not loved people and Jesus like He wanted me to.

I wept over my carnality and over my lack of regard for the people that Jesus had purchased with His own blood. I felt as if Jesus had taken my heart out of my chest, crushed it, and broken it in a million pieces.

I made a vow to God that day that I would love people, I would never say an unkind thing about people, I would do my best to let grace fill my mouth, and I would do my best to always believe the best of everyone, speaking good things over them.

My Life Changes

I may not be batting a thousand yet in my life, but my batting average is a lot higher today than it was then. You can't imagine the change this vision made in my life.

I fell in love with everyone. Oh, glory to God, *everyone!* I had a desire to hug all the babies and kiss all the kids. I became a love fanatic.

One Sunday morning in our church I announced, "If you're a single adult, I'd like you to come to my house for dinner this Friday night."

Much to my joy, a hundred singles showed up for dinner. You talk about wall-to-wall flesh. We had bodies everywhere. You couldn't walk through the house. We have a grand piano in our living room, and the group sang, laughed, cried, and had the greatest time fellowshipping around it.

At midnight, as the last single was trying to leave the house, I was holding onto his arm, saying, "You can't leave! You don't understand: You're Jesus to me. You can't leave. You're my key to being developed in the love of God. Apart from being developed in the love of God, I cannot know Jesus because He is love."

He probably had no idea what I was talking about and thought I had struck out once too often. But my heart had been crushed, and now there was an overwhelming desire in my heart to love people, glorify the Lord, and know Jesus.

My Picture of Jesus

I have known the audible voice of God, but I don't want God to have to shout at me every time He wants my attention. I want to know Jesus so well I will hear Him if He chooses to whisper. And I want to see Jesus in every child of God.

He's there. Every Christian I've ever met represents a part of the fellowship God has ordained for my life. Each of them represents a certain facet of the Lord's character. My picture of Jesus is not complete without them, because I can see Jesus in each of them.

But I've learned through the years that it really takes a lot of work to stay in love with some people. Yet they are the people I really need.

Like you, I've known disappointment in life. I've known broken relationships. People have said things against me and have tried to undermine the work I've given my life for. I've had to stand against bitterness, and I've had to stand against the temptation to render evil for evil.

Several years ago, I went through a particularly difficult situation. I felt violated, betrayed, and hurt, and I didn't want to see or talk to the people who had hurt me. But the Lord kept telling me, "Tom, you can't live this way. You can't be this way. You're going to have to trust again."

Resisting Bitterness

In my heart of hearts, although I was the one who was violated, I knew I was going to have to seek these people out and right the wrong. I didn't feel they could come to me. I felt I was going to have to be big enough to go to them.

I remember picking up the telephone and dialing their number. I said to both of them, "If I've ever said anything to hurt you, forgive me. If I've ever done anything that's offended or hindered you, I'm sorry.

"I sense a great need to walk with you again as a brother. I want to be for you in the Spirit. Let's be reconciled. Let's walk together as one. I want to pray for you. I want to support you. I want to love you. I want to see you prosper in the things of God. I want God to use you for His glory."

You can't imagine how freeing that was. I can honestly say there is not a person on the face of the Earth that I have anything against. I have resolved every difficulty. I have resisted every temptation to be angry and bitter.

I recognize that I am a debtor to every man, and not just to those who are for me, or those who have been kind to me. I owe every person that debt of love, and I know that unless I'm merciful, loving, and forgiving, I'm not correctly related to the Lord.

Putting Love to the Test

Love is going to be put to the test. Jesus was put to the test. Think about Jesus: He healed the sick, raised the dead, fed hungry people, loved people, blessed children, preached the kingdom of God, and met the financial needs of people.

And yet the people of ancient Palestine crucified Jesus. They chose Barabbas over Jesus. Barabbas was the Al Capone of his day. Although he was a notorious criminal, the people chose to free him rather than the Altogether-Lovely-One.

When Jesus was on the Cross of Calvary, He looked into the faces of that angry mob of people who had beaten Him and put Him on that Cross. Can you imagine what He saw as He looked into the eyes of people whose lives were completely taken over by the madness of sin—people completely given over to satanic power?

"Father, Forgive Them"

The Word of God says Jesus had the power, the right, and the ability to call more than twelve legions of angels to rescue Him. (A legion in the Roman army consisted of 3,000 to 6,000 infantry troops and 100 to 200 cavalry troops. Just think how many angels that would have been!)

Jesus could have easily said, "Father, send twelve legions of angels and rescue Me from these evil people!" But He didn't. Instead, He said, "Father, forgive them, for they know not what they do" (Luke 23:34).

Had Jesus gone into the tomb with unforgiveness in His heart, we wouldn't be here today. When He forgave them and us, He disarmed every principality and power. He made an open show of them, triumphing over them in the Cross. He led captivity captive and gave gifts to men (Colossians 2:13-15 and Ephesians 4:8).

By taking our sins on the Cross, Jesus became accursed. He was cast out of the presence of God for you and me. He suffered the torments of our punishment for three days and three nights for you and me.

Men Who Would Be Martyrs

Stephen was the first martyr of the early Church. While he was being stoned to death by the religious leaders of that day, he prayed, "Lord, lay not this sin to their charge" (Acts 7:60).

In Romans 9:3, Paul says that he would be willing to go to hell, to be accursed, and to be separated from God for all eternity if it would mean the salvation of his Jewish brethren. He, too, was willing to forgive those who had persecuted him with such hatred.

To walk in the intimate knowledge of Jesus Christ, we must make a similar commitment of our lives to the people we fellowship with—a commitment to love and serve them when they're good and when they're not so good. The Bible says love hardly ever notices a wrong suffered.

Love does not keep score.

Love does not seek vengeance.

8

Love Never Fails

Though I speak with the tongues of men and of angels, and have not charity [love], I am become as sounding brass, or a tinkling cymbal.

And though I have the gift of prophecy, and understand all mysteries, and all knowledge; and though I have all faith, so that I could remove mountains, and have not charity, I am nothing.

And though I bestow all my goods to feed the poor, and though I give my body to be burned, and have not charity, it profiteth me nothing.

Charity suffereth long, and is kind; charity envieth not; charity vaunteth not itself, is not puffed up,

Doth not behave itself unseemly, seeketh not her own, is not easily provoked, thinketh no evil;

Rejoiceth not in iniquity, but rejoiceth in the truth;

Beareth all things, believeth all things, hopeth all things, endureth all things.

THE REVELATION OF JESUS

> Charity never faileth; but whether there be prophecies, they shall fail; whether there be tongues, they shall cease; whether there be knowledge, it shall vanish away.
>
> For we know in part, and we prophesy in part.
>
> But when that which is perfect is come, then that which is in part shall be done away.
>
> When I was a child, I spake as a child, I understood as a child, I thought as a child: but when I became a man, I put away childish things.
>
> For now we see through a glass, darkly; but then face to face: now I know in part; but then shall I know even as also I am known.
>
> And now abideth faith, hope, charity, these three; but the greatest of these is charity.
>
> 1 Corinthians 13:1-13

Paul says that *agape* (Christian love) always sees the other person as valuable and precious.

Agape never betrays the other person.

Agape is always loyal to the other person.

Agape always sees the other person just as the Lord sees that person.

Making a Lot of Noise

Notice particularly the first verse: "Though I speak with the tongues of men and of angels, and have not charity [love], I am become as sounding brass, or a tinkling cymbal."

In other words, without love, I'm just making a lot of noise.

Have you ever heard someone who wasn't operating in the love of God jump up and prophesy to the church? Their words grate on you because their words are without love.

Paul writes in verses 2 and 3:

> And though I have the gift of prophecy, and understand all mysteries, and all knowledge; and though I have all faith, so that I could remove mountains, and have not charity, I am nothing.
>
> And though I bestow all my goods to feed the poor, and though I give my body to be burned, and have not charity, it profiteth me nothing.

Think of it! Understanding every mystery of God, possessing all knowledge, having the faith to move mountains, even giving my body to be burned—yet, if love is not motivating me, what I have done means nothing in the sight of God.

Paul continues, "Agape suffers long." When was the last time we were long-suffering—patient—when someone dealt a blow to us?

Agape is kind.

Agape does not envy.

Agape does not boast, it is not proud.

Agape is not rude, it is not self-seeking, it is not easily angered.

Agape never keeps record of wrongs.

Agape does not delight in evil, but rejoices in the truth.

Agape always protects, always trusts, always hopes, always perseveres.

Agape never fails.

Perfect Love

> But whether there be prophecies, they shall fail; whether there be tongues, they shall cease; whether there be knowledge, it shall vanish away.
>
> For we know in part, and we prophesy in part.
>
> But when that which is perfect is come, then that which is in part shall be done away.
>
> 1 Corinthians 13:8-10

We need to understand that love enables us to see clearly, not in part. Love causes us to do things the right way. When that which is perfect (love is perfect because God is love) fills our hearts we see differently, we hear differently, we act differently—we actually begin to see, hear, and act like Jesus.

Jesus did not do His work in part. Why not? Because He was walking in the love of God. Love never fails; love is never selfish; love enables us to do it God's way. Jesus told us, "Love your enemies, bless them that curse you, do good to them that hate you, and pray for them which despitefully use you, and persecute you; That ye may be the children of your Father which is in heaven: . . . Be ye therefore perfect, even as your Father which is in heaven is perfect" (Matthew 5:44-45, 48). How can we be perfect? Through love.

Childish Things

In 1 Corinthians 13:11, Paul continues, "When I was a child, I spake as a child, I understood as a child, I thought as a child: but when I became a man, I put away childish things."

Here Paul is talking about becoming a mature Christian. What are some of the childish things Paul put away? When he wrote his first letter to the Corinthian church, he listed some of these childish things in the third chapter.

He said, in effect, "There are divisions among you. There are factions in this church. I wanted to preach the full counsel of God—I wanted to feed you with meat—yet I could not do so, for where there is envy, strife, and division are you not still carnal, babes in Christ, still needing the milk of the Word?"

There are some Christians who will fight with you at the proverbial "drop of a hat." And there are some Christians who, if they are not the actual source of gossip themselves, cluster around every gossiper in a church—and every church has its own "Sister Bucketmouth" who seems intent on continually causing strife.

Paul speaks effectively to that kind of person in 1 Corinthians 3:1, "It's spiritual people who judge all things; and I could not speak unto you as spiritual, but as unto carnal, because you are still babes in Christ."

As long as we bear the characteristics of a carnal person, we close our eyes and our hearts to revelation, and God cannot enlighten the eyes of our spiritual understanding.

Paul's Prayer for the Ephesians

When Paul wrote to the church at Ephesus, he stated in the first chapter that he had heard about their faith and their love for the saints of God—and that because of that he was praying for them. He wrote:

> Wherefore I also, after I heard of your faith in the Lord Jesus, and love unto all the saints,
>
> Cease not to give thanks for you, making mention of you in my prayers;
>
> That the God of our Lord Jesus Christ, the Father of glory, may give unto you the spirit of wisdom and revelation in the knowledge of him:
>
> The eyes of your understanding being enlightened; that ye may know what is the hope of his calling, and what the riches of the glory of his inheritance in the saints,
>
> And what is the exceeding greatness of his power toward us who believe . . .
>
> Ephesians 1:15-19

But carnal Christians cannot walk in that kind of knowledge, because they have closed their lives to it.

Through a Glass Darkly

Paul concludes the great love chapter with these words: "For now we see through a glass darkly; but then face to face: now I know in part; but then shall I know even as also I am known" (1 Corinthians 13:12). When is "then"? Is it in the sweet by-and-by? No! "Then" is when you and I start walking in the love of God.

> And now abideth faith, hope, charity, these three; but the greatest of these is charity [love].
>
> 1 Corinthians 13:13

Do you realize what Paul is saying here? He is saying that the eyes of the recreated human spirit—the spiritual senses of the new creation in Christ Jesus—are faith, hope, and charity. He is saying, don't wait until you get to heaven to see Him, but let faith fill your hearts. Faith believes that *He is*, not will be or could be, but that *He is*—He is your healer, provider, refuge, savior, friend, high tower, and champion. You must live by faith, for without faith it is impossible to please Him (Hebrews 11:6).

You must also keep hope alive in your heart. The apostle John points out in 1 John 3:3 that the man who has this hope purifies himself—and Hebrews 12:24 says that without holiness no man shall see the Lord.

These verses are in keeping with what Jesus said in Matthew 5:8, "Blessed are the pure in heart: for they shall see God."

Walking in Love

Paul said, in essence, "Keep yourself in love, for God is love, and love never fails." And John wrote, "We know that whosoever is born of God sinneth not; but he that is begotten of God keepeth himself, and that wicked one toucheth him not" (1 John 5:18). That's why Jesus said of Himself, "the prince of this world cometh, and hath nothing in me" (John 14:30). The Amplified (AMP) version of this verse shows its meaning in detail, and shows why Satan could do nothing to Jesus:

> I will not talk with you much more, for the prince (evil genius, ruler) of this world is coming. And he

has no claim on me—he has nothing in common with Me, there is nothing in Me that belongs to him, he has no power over Me.

All this was because Jesus never stepped outside of divine love. He never stepped out of *agape*. He never stepped out of anything that would violate the love of God. As Paul states about faith, hope, and charity, "the greatest of these is charity [the love of God]." *The greatest of all is love!*

Riddles and Mysteries

Here's my version of what Paul said in 1 Corinthians 13:12. "I have put away childish things, and I have become a man. I am living by the senses of my recreated spirit. I am looking into a glass darkly. I am looking into a riddle. I am looking into a mystery. I know in part now, but that riddle, that mystery, is becoming clearer to me—because love opens my eyes to see as He sees.

Do you know who stands on the other side of that glass? Jesus! When we see Jesus, we shall be like Him. The clearer the mystery, the clearer the revelation of Jesus Christ.

Do you know something else? You need other Christians. You can't make it without them. Furthermore, I can't make it without them, and I wouldn't even want to try to make it without them, because they are bone of my bone and flesh of my flesh—and collectively we are bone of Jesus' bone and we are flesh of His flesh. When I reach out in love toward another Christian, I'm reaching out toward Jesus Christ.

The Most Important Principle

I have just given you what I believe is the most important principle in all of God's Word. It's not having faith for another Christian or even for yourself—it's having faith for the *Body of Christ.*

It's not saying, "Lord, use me in the gifts of the Holy Spirit." It's saying, "Lord, regardless of whom You choose to use, let the gifts be in manifestation so we all might profit from them."

The love of God is the foundation upon which Christianity can build—indeed, *must* build. If we don't build upon this foundation, there will be cracks in the foundation. The love of God is the only foundation that will last, for that foundation is Jesus Christ Himself, the Chief Cornerstone of the glorious Church.

Seeing Jesus

Look around in your church. Smile real big. You'd better realize by now that you're looking at Jesus Christ! I don't care what you call that person—it may be John, Betty, or Sandra—you're actually looking at Jesus Christ, at His Body on this Earth. And God measures the love that you have for Him by the love you have for that person sitting next to you.

This is why the Body of Christ has not yet seen the Lord clearly and why our words somehow tend to be empty and in vain. Outsiders may not say it to our faces, but they're thinking it: "I can't hear what you're saying because your life is speaking too loudly."

THE REVELATION OF JESUS

After my grandmother went to be with the Lord, I found this written in the flyleaf of her Bible: "Your life is the only Bible that a careless world will read. What if the type is crooked? What if the ink is blurred?"

The New Commandment

Jesus said, "A new commandment I give unto you" (John 13:34). The new commandment was,". . . love one another, as I have loved you." Then He continued in the next verse, "By this shall all men know that ye are my disciples, if ye have love one to another."

God's Word tells us that we are "lively [living] stones" (1 Peter 2:5). We need to make certain, therefore, that we fit—that we are properly aligned with the rest of the family of God.

There's a lot of work we need to do on ourselves. We need to take sandpaper, a saw, a hammer, and a chisel and smooth ourselves out. We can take our dimensions from Jesus, the Chief Cornerstone.

If We Really Knew Jesus

How well do we really know Jesus Christ? Come on. How well do we really *know* the Lord? I'm convinced if we really knew Him as we think we know Him, we wouldn't live the way we live.

If we really knew the Lord as we profess to know Him, we wouldn't do the things we do. We wouldn't say the things we say. We wouldn't watch the television programs and videos that we watch.

If we really knew the Lord as we say we know Him, we would have a much greater commitment to the Body of Christ. We wouldn't be able to rest if we knew that a brother or a sister was in need. We would try to move heaven and Earth on that person's behalf.

If we really knew the Lord as we say we know the Lord, we would pray for the people of God. And we would be in church during special services instead of sitting somewhere feeding our face and watching television—sticking junk food into our body and trash TV into our soul.

We would be saying, "Lord, I can't eat while there is a brother or a sister in need. I will set food aside and fast to seek Your face on their behalf. Lord, I can't rest until I see Your blessing and provision at work in that person's life. Lord, I will sanctify myself for Your work."

That's how Jesus began His public ministry: He spent the first 40 days in fasting and in prayer.

Empowered by the Spirit

The Bible says that Jesus was led of the Spirit into the wilderness to be tempted by Satan (Luke 4:1-13). When the enemy came against Him, He overcame him with the Word of God. After Satan concluded his temptation, he left Jesus "for a season."

Leaving the wilderness and returning to Galilee, Jesus began ministering in the power of the Spirit, and His fame began to spread. His life from that point on was devoted to meeting the needs of the people.

How well do we really know the Lord? Have our lives really been transfigured, transformed? On a scale of one to a million, where do we stand today? Probably at about minus one.

It's little wonder we have such a difficult time hearing the voice of God. It's little wonder that the words of Jesus are so difficult for us to understand. Having ears, we can't hear; having eyes, we can't see.

Knowing Jesus

There's a lot of work I need to do on myself, and I'm going to do it. With God's help, I'm going to do it, because the cry of my heart is to know Jesus Christ!

Paul said it so well: "That I may know him, and the power of his resurrection, and the fellowship of his sufferings, being made conformable unto his death" (Philippians 3:10).

In verse 8, he expressed the same longing: "I count all things but loss for the excellency of the knowledge of Christ Jesus my Lord: for whom I have suffered the loss of all things, and do count them but dung, that I may win Christ."

Paul gave up his pride and his selfishness—everything he held dear—that he might know Christ. To Paul, the things of this world were dung compared with the excellency of knowing Jesus Christ.

Jesus Knocks at Our Heart's Door

Jesus stands at the door of our hearts, just as He once stood at the door of Paul's heart. In Revelation 3:20, Jesus said, in effect, "Behold, I stand at the door and knock. Can you hear My voice? Can you hear Me knocking? It's not a stranger calling you. My sheep know My voice, and a stranger's voice they will not follow.

"Behold, I stand at the door of your house, and I knock; and if any man hear My voice and open the door, I will come in to him, and I will sup with him.

"The thing that My heart loves more than anything else is to be together with you and to have fellowship with you. I want to have an intimate, personal relationship with you. I will sup with you, and you with Me."

Some of us are so hardheaded, the Lord has to almost knock the door down.

How God Measures Your Love

Your commitment to other Christians is your commitment to Jesus. My commitment to Christians like you is my commitment to the Lord.

The love Christians have for each other is the level of the love they have for Jesus Christ. The love you have for the people of your local church is the level of your commitment to the Lord.

That's how God measures it, so you'd better find a place of service. You'd better get involved in what God is doing in your church.

When your pastor stands up and announces, "We need men and women to help with the ushering program of the church, and also men and women to work with our children," you'd better respond.

To close your heart to that need is to close your heart to Jesus. When you walk into the church nursery, Jesus says to you, "When you receive this child in My Name, you're not just receiving this child, you're receiving a much greater realm of fellowship. You're not just receiving Me, you're receiving the Father as well. But if you say no, you're saying no to Me."

THE REVELATION OF JESUS

Remember, at the conclusion of the Last Supper, Jesus took a basin of water, girded Himself with a towel, and began to wash His disciples' feet—and the servant is not greater than his or her Lord.

Next time you're at your church, take a chance and look at someone and tell them, "I've decided I'm going to out-love you. I'm going to love you more than you love me. I'm going to serve you in a greater way than you serve me."